How Are We Doing?

**A 1-Hour Guide to
Evaluating Your Performance
as a Nonprofit Board**

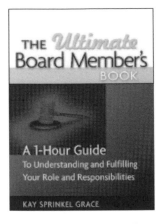

The Ultimate Board Member's Book, by Kay Sprinkel Grace

Here is a book for all nonprofit boards:

• Those wanting to operate with maximum effectiveness,

• Those needing to clarify exactly what their job is, and,

• Those wanting to ensure that all members – novice and veteran alike – are "on the same page" with respect to roles and responsibilities.

The Ultimate Board Member's Book takes only 60 minutes to read, yet it provides a solid command of just what you need to do to help your organization succeed.

It's all here in jargon-free language: how boards work, what the job entails, the time commitment, the role of staff, serving on committees and task forces, fundraising responsibilities, conflicts of interest, group decision-making, how to develop yourself, effective recruiting, de-enlisting board members, board self-evaluation, and more.

The Ultimate Board Member's Book is "real world" not theoretical. It focuses on issues and concerns that all board members will inevitably face and equips you with the skills to master them.

www.emersonandchurch.com

How Are We Doing?

A 1-Hour Guide to
Evaluating Your Performance
as a Nonprofit Board

Gayle L. Gifford

Emerson
& Church
PUBLISHERS

This text is printed on acid-free paper.

10 9 8 7 6 5 4 3

Printed in the United States of America

Copies of this book are available from the publisher at discount when purchased in quantity for boards of directors or staff.

First printed May 2005

ISBN: 1-889102-23-7

Emerson & Church, Publishers
P.O. Box 338, Medfield, MA 02052
Tel. 508-359-0019 • Fax 508-359-2703
www.emersonandchurch.com

Library of Congress Cataloging-in-Publication Data

Gifford, Gayle L.
  How are we doing? : a 1-hour guide to evaluating your performance as a nonprofit board / Gayle L. Gifford.
       p. cm.
    ISBN 1-889102-23-7 (pbk. : alk. paper)
    1. Nonprofit organizations--Management. I. Title.
    HD62.6.G474 2005
    658'.048--dc22
                                            2005001349

CONTENTS

Part III: Building a Great Board

INTRODUCTION

Philanthropy is a gift. From its Greek root, meaning "love of humankind," it embodies the best of humanity voluntary acts of service for the common good.

The way most people practice philanthropy today is through a special class of organizations called "non-profit."

These organizations, because of their role in improving our communities, are accorded a host of privileges by the government:

• Nonprofit organizations don't pay taxes on much of the income they receive.

• Donors receive a tax deduction for contributions made to a special category of nonprofits known as 501(c)3s in the tax code .

• Nonprofits can use the unpaid services of volunteers and not run afoul of labor laws.

Interestingly, nonprofit organizations don't belong to any one person or group of people. Instead, their assets are "owned" by society as a whole. In fact, when a nonprofit is dissolved, its property must be distributed to another nonprofit.

To ensure that these special organizations meet their

moral and legal responsibilities, they are entrusted – thus the word, 'trustee' – to the individuals who serve on their boards.

Which brings me to you.

Your two principal charges as a nonprofit board are to "serve the common good" and "to protect the assets of your organization." And the decisions you make while carrying out your duties can, and often do, affect people's lives dramatically. In other words, this is serious business.

With such a load to shoulder, you might expect to undergo hours of rigorous training – a sort of "director's ed" to help you steer the proper course.

But the reality is, most of us simply jump behind the wheel and learn on the job. What training we do receive is usually patchwork rather than formal.

As a consequence, not only are there swerves and hazards along the way, but it can be difficult to judge just what kind of job your board is doing.

This book is an attempt to change that.

In my view, your performance as a board is measured against three yardsticks:

1) How will you make the community better?
2) How good a steward are you?
3) How well do you work as a team?

Those are the big issues and if you look at the Contents page, you'll see I've organized this book to reflect them.

You've chosen to generously devote yourself to an important cause. What you deserve in turn is the opportunity to experience the extraordinary joy of philanthropic service.

A Personal Note on Using This Book

*They say that time changes things, but you
actually have to change them yourself.*
– Andy Warhol

If you're reading this book, you have already asked
the essential question: How can we be a better board?

But after you've turned the final page, what then?
How can you best use what you've learned to influence
your board and improve the impact of your organization?

Probably the simplest way is to start a casual conversation with your fellow directors on the points you find
most compelling. I know from my own experience on
boards that just one director asking questions can spark
a chain of discussions that can have a profound influence.

Another way to use this book is more structured. It
might serve as the core of your board retreat or special
meeting, where a point by point discussion takes place,
perhaps with the aid of a facilitator.

Those are just two possibilities. No doubt you and
your board will think of other variations.

Each of the 34 brief chapters, beginning with "Does
our vision matter?" is in the form of a straightforward

question, designed to get right to the heart of your practice.

While I could have added more chapters, and more questions, I have winnowed the list to cover the most pressing issues in evaluating your board.

You'll find, at the end of each chapter, a small box labeled, "Your Evaluation." Here, you're asked to assess your own board in light of what you've just read. I've placed the boxes in this way so that the ideas presented will still be fresh in your mind. I've also included the entire content of these boxes in the Appendix.

Two points in closing.

You cannot of course implement every change at once – if you try, your directors will become frustrated and slip back into old ways. Patience and persistence are required.

Lastly, whether you use this book formally or informally isn't nearly as important as the attitude you bring to the whole process of evaluation.

If you have an open mind, a caring heart, and the willingness to apply a tad of elbow grease, you and your fellow directors can indeed build a strong and respected organization capable of making the world a better place for all.

–GLG

PART I

MAKING OUR COMMUNITY BETTER

"No pessimist ever discovered the secrets
of the stars, or sailed to uncharted land,
or opened a new doorway for the human spirit."

Helen Keller

1 ☑

Does our vision matter?

Imagine those first days of your organization. Can you see your founders, sitting around a kitchen table or in someone's living room?

Do you hear them speaking, passionate about the world as it could be, outraged at what is? Tirelessly working day and night, despite overwhelming obstacles, in service to their cause, hungry to make a difference.

What brought them together? In all likelihood, they shared powerful dreams...

- They saw people who were hungry and decided to feed them.
- They saw people stricken by disease and decided to heal them.
- They saw a river burning and decided to make it clean again.
- They saw a community in silence and decided to bring it music.
- They saw their heritage being lost and decided to preserve it.

Your founders dreamed of a better world and believed

they had the ability to achieve that dream – or at least to try. If today you asked your fellow directors why *they* serve, would they echo the passionate fire of your founding vision?

Or would they describe the board's role in mundane terms – attending meetings, watching the finances, raising money, creating policy, supervising the CEO?

While those routine tasks are important duties of boards, they only make sense as a means to achieving your greater vision. It's not enough to outfit and command a tight little ship. That ship has to deliver its passengers to their desired destination or you've failed your mission.

Throughout this book, you'll encounter phrases like *meaningful difference, community change, work that matters*. Ultimately, your performance as a board isn't judged by the health of your balance sheet, or the sparkle of your facility, no matter how important these may be.

The true measure is the difference you make – call it your mission or true calling – in the lives you save, the natural resources you protect, the beauty you enhance, or the spiritual solace you provide.

Whatever you do, achieving that vision is what matters.

YOUR EVALUATION

1. Our board has articulated a vision and mission that are important today.

__ Strongly Agree __ Agree __ Disagree __ Strongly Disagree

---

2 ☑

Have we set a goal
for the good we can do?

*How will our community be better because of what
we do?*

That doesn't sound like such a tough question, but
for many boards it's the hardest one to answer. And the
most important.

Many boards hedge when asked to set goals describing how their community will be better off. It's tempting
to think about your organization only in terms of what
you are – a community center or a school, for example.
And then to judge your effectiveness on that basis – *did
we put on lots of interesting programs? Is our building
clean?*

But the impact of that community center is much
greater than buildings and activities. It brings the
generations together. It's a safe space where children and
the elderly can thrive. It rekindles community spirit, the
arts, culture, and recreation.

These are the results that matter, the ways in which

our lives are enriched. What is it that you want to achieve for your community? Until you know, you won't be able to design the best programs to get you there.

Here's an example. The board of a small community land trust saw its primary purpose as building public support for land conservation. While it had acquired 400 acres of protected lands in its first 10 years, its goals were largely to expand membership and run education programs.

But with the prodding of a few major supporters, the board decided to undertake a rigorous self-examination. What difference are we making? they asked. Are we doing enough?

The answer to that question was – we can do more. So the board set a bold new goal – to permanently protect 2000 acres of land. This new focus led to a restructuring that produced astounding results. In the next four years it *more than doubled* its protected holdings.

Often boards are reluctant to quantify the community impact they desire because they're afraid of falling short of the goal.

But if your vision isn't bold enough to matter, it probably won't inspire others to action. And while it may be a cliché, it's nevertheless true that you won't get to your destination if you don't know where you are going.

YOUR EVALUATION

2. Our board has defined concrete results for the community change we will hold ourselves accountable for.

__ Strongly Agree __ Agree __ Disagree __ Strongly Disagree

---

3 ☑

How well do we know our community's needs?

In business, you'd be hard pressed to convince anyone to invest money in your company if you couldn't describe the size, characteristics and needs of your market.

Business investors need confidence that company managers know what they're doing. They want to know their investment will result in some significant returns for the money they put in.

Your community investors expect the same of your organization. There is no excuse for a board not knowing the basics of its core business.

Imagine you were starting an organization to help a recent wave of refugees coming to town. What would you want to know?

You'd talk to immigration officials to find out who was coming, how many, how old, how needy. You'd talk to realtors to learn about housing. You'd visit business leaders to learn about jobs. You'd talk to school officials about enrollment and special services.

And, then, if you were really thorough, you'd take it a step further. You'd learn about the culture, traditions and values of the refugees. You'd contact other agencies to find out what services they could provide. You'd visit potential donors to assess the likelihood of financial support. You'd meet with government and elected officials.

Understanding the scope of community need is an essential part of every board's work, whether you're the board of a start-up organization or an established one.

Responsible boards yearn for information that will allow them to focus on the most pressing needs of their constituents. Without it, it's difficult to direct resources to where they can make the greatest difference.

Not that keeping up with community change is easy. It means talking with service providers, seeking advice from community leaders, meeting with government officials, even reading data and conducting surveys.

"Fine, we'll put the staff right on it," I hear you say. That's tempting, I admit. But your constituents want to see and talk to *you*, the people in charge.

And besides, there are genuine benefits to doing the work yourself. Not only will you gain insights into your community, you'll experience firsthand how your organization is perceived, and maybe even identify a promising candidate for the board.

YOUR EVALUATION

3. Our board regularly conducts or reviews research to gain a better understanding of our community and its needs.

__ Strongly Agree __ Agree __ Disagree __ Strongly Disagree

---

4 ☑️

Do shared values guide our practices?

Most of us know the Golden Rule. This simple code – *do to others as you would have them do to you* – is a powerful moral guide.

If you lived by the Golden Rule, you'd never lie or cheat or steal or inflict harm on others. You'd be an exceptional role model.

Statements of guiding beliefs such as the Golden Rule, the Ten Commandments, or the Pillars of Islam, set expectations and limitations for their followers.

But you don't have to be a religious institution to benefit from a moral code. Nonprofits, government, and businesses can also benefit from a set of guiding values.

Examples are all around us. The *Geneva Conventions* set standards for the conduct of nations. Professional associations require their members to sign a code of ethics. Some retailers even post their values for customers to see – for example, *We do not test our products or ingredients on animals.*

The public expects nonprofit organizations to practice what they preach. Imagine the fallout for an environmental group fined for polluting. Or how quickly the media would eviscerate a nonprofit serving people with disabilities if its annual meeting were held in a facility lacking wheelchair access.

Value statements define what you believe and guide your actions. They codify shared beliefs and keep staff and board moving in the same direction.

In writing your statement, articulate what makes you different from organizations that look similar. For example,

> *Our child care center encourages children's independence, or, We believe that strict discipline is essential to a child's growth.*

Are there spiritual or scientific beliefs that guide your work? For example,

> *Our school upholds Quaker values, or, Science grounds all of our actions.*

Some include commitments to inclusion and accessibility:

> *Our services are open to all in need, regardless of their beliefs.*

Others restrict participation:

> *We do not accept donations that could compromise our independence or integrity.*

What is key is that you examine your own organization and identify its bedrock beliefs, what you hold most dear.

If you haven't worked on a values statement yet, you'll find the discussion enlightening. Many boards are surprised to find differences of opinion on what they think are shared beliefs.

If you already have a values statement, is it still meaningful? And, most importantly, are the values reflected in everything you do?

YOUR EVALUATION

4. Our board has clearly articulated the values that guide our decisions and actions.

__ Strongly Agree __ Agree __ Disagree __ Strongly Disagree

5

Are we prepared to respond to a changing world?

The March of Dimes could have dissolved when the polio vaccine made its original purpose virtually obsolete. Instead, it expanded its mission to focus on preventing three great risks to healthy babies – birth defects, premature birth and low birth weight – continuing to make an important contribution to all of us.

Your organization may not experience a change as dramatic. But consider some of the changes you've personally witnessed in your own community:

- Businesses closing, merging, or opening.
- Changes in political or community leadership.
- Shifts or cutbacks in state or federal spending.
- An influx of refugees as a result of distant wars.
- New technologies transforming the workplace.

Because no organization is immune to these changes, a vibrant board needs to keep its eyes and ears wide open. It stays constantly alert to trends, issues, and crises that may immediately or eventually affect its mission, its constituents or the revenues it depends on.

Unfortunately, many boards only talk about changes in the community every few years when someone dusts off the old strategic plan and says it's time for a new one.

There are many ways to keep your board apprised of important changes. For example, directors and staff of state humanities councils gather each spring in Washington for "Humanities on the Hill" to meet Congressional representatives and discuss issues of local and national importance – and then report to their board when they return.

An AIDS Service Organization annually asks someone from the state health department to brief its board on funding changes and emerging health concerns.

Community foundations frequently hold public forums where directors can learn from local, state or even national experts.

And there's always the tried and true – reading newspapers and journals to keep abreast of changes.

Is your board thinking about the future? Have you developed good radar to be alerted to important shifts in your community or the resources you depend on?

Great boards not only monitor change, they prepare for it.

YOUR EVALUATION

5. Our board regularly considers the effects that outside changes could have on the organization.

__ Strongly Agree __ Agree __ Disagree __ Strongly Disagree

6

Do we think and act strategically?

How do we put a park in walking distance of every American child?

The Trust for Public Land (TPL), a land conservation organization, challenged itself with that question. On its face, the answer seemed fairly obvious – raise money to buy land and set it aside for parks. But it turns out the solution wasn't that simple.

TPL's research, which was thorough, showed that city kids were desperately in need of parks. But financially-strapped municipal park departments were unwilling to take on new parks they couldn't afford to maintain. And communities weren't interested in introducing more neglected property into their neighborhoods.

TPL's response addressed the question at the heart of all strategic thinking: *How can we create the breakthrough needed to achieve our goal?*

Now, with its "Parks for People" program, TPL is determined to achieve that breakthrough by presenting a more compelling case for urban parks, providing cities with best practices for excellent parks, and serving as a catalyst for land acquisition and private and public fundraising.

What strategic thinking does, as the TPL example shows, is shatter the tired lament, "We've always done it this way." It searches instead for bold new solutions. It envisions change ... and questions sacred cows:

- How can we do more of what makes us successful?
- How can we dismantle the barriers standing in our way? Can we go around them?
- What is too farfetched to consider? Is there a way this could happen?
- How can we control our future instead of being passive bystanders?

With strategic thinking, breakthroughs emerge, such as when hunger advocates created sophisticated networks to rescue wasted food and deliver it to people in need. Or when preservationists and environmentalists created the smart growth movement, tieing the conservation of rural areas to successful city revitalization.

Strategic thinking is a mindset, a perspective, a way of seeing the world. As such, it shouldn't be limited to those prescribed years when you come together to create a formal strategic plan.

The best boards think strategically as a matter of course. They're ready to respond to changing circumstances as they focus unrelentingly on achieving their vision and mission.

YOUR EVALUATION

6. Our board regularly discusses how to create breakthroughs.

__ Strongly Agree __ Agree __ Disagree __ Strongly Disagree

---

7 ☑️

Do we know if our programs are having an impact?

With billions of dollars contributed to nonprofit organizations each year, more donors are questioning how much return they're getting on that investment.

Government, private funders, and the public want to see results. This push for accountability is good for our organizations. But being accountable for *results* isn't a simple undertaking for most organizations.

Consider the firestorm around educational testing in public schools. Whatever you believe about its merits, there are important and fundamental questions at its center:

What do we want our kids to know and be able to do? How do we know they are learning? Who are we failing and why? What are we getting for our investment?

Yes, evaluation is tough. Yes, progress is hard to

measure. Yes, some funders set unrealistic timelines to deliver results.

But no matter how hard, if your board isn't trying to measure results, then you can't be confident the money you spend is having any impact at all.

For three decades, Save The Bay has been the public champion of a clean and healthy Narragansett Bay.

Sewage and toxic pollution have fallen significantly. But pollution levels, directors knew, aren't a complete measure of the Bay's ecological health.

After considerable deliberation, the organization developed a "State of the Bay" report that, over time, monitors changes in ten categories, ranging from eelgrass to fisheries. Now, the board can focus on the systems most in need of repair and spot new problems as they emerge.

If your board hasn't seriously examined your organization's impact, try stimulating interest by asking the questions that lie at the heart of any evaluation:

- *What's working?* – So you can keep doing the things that produce results.

- *How do we know?* – Because your evaluation should be based on evidence, not just a few nice stories.

- *What isn't working?* – So you can stop doing it.

- *Why is it or isn't it working?* – So you can learn how to do better.

It's tempting to keep doing what you've always

done. But people's lives and your donor's contributions are at stake. It's negligent to keep investing money in programs without proof they make a difference.

YOUR EVALUATION

7. Our board is able to measure whether our organization is having a significant impact on the community.

__ Strongly Agree   __ Agree   __ Disagree   __ Strongly Disagree

---

PART II

BECOMING GOOD STEWARDS

"A little neglect may breed great mischief;
for want of a nail the shoe was lost; for want
of a shoe the horse was lost; and for want
of a horse the rider was lost...."

Benjamin Franklin

8 ☑

What kind of stewards are we?

It's time to shift focus to the second part of a board's job.

So far, you've examined how well you're serving your community. Now it's time to consider how good a steward you are.

Steward is a wonderful word to describe a nonprofit board. A steward is someone hired to care for and manage another person's estate or property.

It couldn't be more fitting to apply this evocative word to your board. As directors, you don't own your organization – it "belongs" to the public and community you serve. Instead, you are entrusted with its care on their behalf.

In your care are the assets of the organization, which include *tangible* items such as your endowment, savings account, buildings, or equipment.

But that's not all. You're also responsible for the *intangible* assets of your organization.

In the for-profit world, intangibles are extremely

valuable assets. Many businesses find that intangibles like expertise or brand identity contribute more to their total worth than equipment or inventory.

Once you start naming the intangible assets of your own organization, you'll recognize just how vital they are for your success.

For example, imagine how difficult it would be to reach your goals if you lost your loyal donors, your tax exempt status, the good will of your community, or the accumulated knowledge and expertise of your staff.

Throughout the next few chapters, you can evaluate how responsible you've been about protecting those assets – tangible and intangible. And that even includes a good look at the board as an asset all by itself.

After you've analyzed your current assets, you'll have a good understanding of the value they bring to your organization – and how *much more* value they could be producing.

Ultimately, you'll want to become *asset-generators*, creating more power to transform the community you serve.

YOUR EVALUATION

8. Our board has identified the tangible and intangible assets of our organization that need to be protected or grown.

__ Strongly Agree __ Agree __ Disagree __ Strongly Disagree

9 ☑

Is our organization trustworthy and worthy of support?

Can your organization pass the *Mom* test?

Let's say your mother came to you for advice: *"Dale, you're well off, your sisters don't need my help. I've decided to leave what money I have to charity. What do you think of my giving it to the group you're involved with?"*

When deciding what to say to your Mom, you would probably ask yourself two questions. The first one is likely to be: Is my organization *worthy* of such a big gift?

With good board stewardship, there should be no doubt that the organization in your care is worthy of support.

You can spot a worthy organization pretty easily:

- Its passionate and competent leaders turn dreams into reality.
- Its cause really matters and its programs change lives.
- It invests its money well, where it generates the greatest impact.

While worthiness is critical, it still isn't enough to meet the Mom test. You can probably think of a few worthy organizations you'd never give to because you don't trust how well they are managed.

Which brings me to the second Mom question: Is this a place my mother can *trust* with her money?

When you honor your responsibility as a steward, you won't settle for anything short of an organization that your donors, your clients, the public and the media know can be trusted.

That means you have to:

- Put ethics and stewardship above all else.
- Deliver on your promises.
- Avoid conflicts of interest and always make decisions in the best interests of the community and people you serve.
- Consider every dollar and every asset a precious resource to be used wisely.

As you evaluate all the many responsibilities of your role as a good steward, keep thinking about your mother. Because if your organization isn't worthy of her support, it isn't worthy of anyone else's either.

YOUR EVALUATION

9. I would feel confident letting my mother make a significant gift to our organization.

__ Strongly Agree __ Agree __ Disagree __ Strongly Disagree

10 ☑

Have we hired
the best CEO for the job?

Have you ever been in a situation at work where everyone was convinced a particular problem was impossible to solve? And then a new person was hired and, suddenly, those seemingly insurmountable barriers melted away?

That's the difference hiring the *right* person can make.

When you consider how much of your organization's success depends on your CEO, it's essential to hire well. Even if you aren't looking for a CEO right now, you probably will be sometime in the future.

So what constitutes the ideal chief executive?

Knowledge, skills, ability and personality are on the list. But that's not all.

Imagine a private technology high school that hires a well-known engineer to be its new head. She wowed the board with her expertise and exciting new ideas.

But as the board soon learns, its new executive doesn't have the political savvy to get her ideas past the faculty senate or the interpersonal skills to generate critical alumni gifts.

What made this individual a great engineer didn't translate into being a great leader. She didn't have what human resource professionals call the right job *"competencies"* – the blend of behaviors and actions built from experience that allow people to perform successfully.

Those same professionals insist that the best way to know what someone can do is to verify what they have already done. Rather than ask candidates to answer hypothetical questions, have them describe real work situations where they personally made a difference. Then check and double check references.

Even if you've done an exhaustive search for the right candidate, you may not have found one person with every quality you desire. Superman hasn't accepted many CEO jobs lately.

In this case, don't compromise those critical leadership competencies – like vision, inspiring others to action, and forging strong teams.

And remember, even a superhero would find it hard to lead an organization where the board meddles in management affairs, strips the CEO of power and authority, or allows its chair to unilaterally direct the CEO or other staff.

YOUR EVALUATION

10. I am confident we have the right CEO for the organization.

__ Strongly Agree __ Agree __ Disagree __ Strongly Disagree

---

11 ☑

Do we regularly evaluate our CEO?

Imagine dinner out in a very posh restaurant. The waiter arrives and you order: "Bring me something interesting to eat and something cold to drink."

The waiter brings your dinner – tripe soup and prune juice. You were imagining something more like Oysters Rockefeller and champagne. You're disappointed and your waiter probably lost a big tip too.

Just like that waiter, it's unfair to evaluate a CEO against unstated criteria. It's also unwise for a board to be so unclear about what it expects.

The only way to set performance standards is to have a frank discussion with your CEO about what's needed and what's possible. In that discussion, you can review your strategic goals, set priorities and clarify the extent to which you'll hold your CEO responsible for achieving results.

Because your CEO's leadership in the office and in the community is so important, you'll want to establish expectations there as well. And reinforce the importance of your CEO serving as a role model for your values.

During your discussion, you can agree on what results are "good enough" (your non-negotiable base) and what's outstanding. Be clear about the connection between compensation and performance. And, you'll also want to agree on what evidence the board will use to document performance.

Performance standards serve as an annual roadmap for both your CEO and your board when you put them in writing. You can do this with an approved business plan, a CEO job plan, or some other tool that reinforces – for everyone involved – that the evaluation will be based on specific criteria, not personal opinion.

While the formal evaluation of CEO performance may happen once a year, good board-CEO partnerships include two-way feedback on performance year-round.

Accountable to all – board, staff, donors, the community – your CEO has one of the toughest jobs around. You can ease some of that stress by setting a clear direction and providing regular feedback on performance.

YOUR EVALUATION

11. Our board has clearly stated its expectations of the CEO and regularly discusses with him or her how well those expectations are being met.

___ Strongly Agree ___ Agree ___ Disagree ___ Strongly Disagree

12 ☑

Have we given our CEO the necessary support?

In the *Rumplestiltskin* fairy tale a poor miller's daughter is locked in a room by the king and told to spin straw into gold upon penalty of death.

Have you done this to your CEO?

Certainly boards hire their chief executives with high hopes for great outcomes. But like the poor miller's daughter, few mortals have gold-spinning powers. Most need some support to achieve great results.

I've often heard CEOs confess that they feel alone and without support running their organizations. "I appreciate their vote of confidence, but I don't feel completely comfortable steering this ship without *some* direction from the board."

And these are chief executives who are highly competent and well respected for running successful organizations.

In surveys conducted across the U.S., most CEOs report that they love their work. Yet, they also lament how they're subject to constant stress, especially from financial and personnel worries. Their days seem never to end, with evenings filled with more meetings and community events.

So when they turn to the board, they often need an antidote to the demands. In other words, a collegial, dedicated, and self-managed team that can offer wise counsel.

Too often they get micromanagers instead, or equally bad, uninterested or unreliable directors who squander their time.

Just what does your CEO need from you, in addition to reasonable compensation, a healthy workplace, and opportunities for professional growth?

Part of the answer lies within yourself: just what would *you* want from the board if you were in the CEO's shoes?

Another part of the answer can be found by talking with your counterparts at other organizations. What needs have they gleaned from their CEOs?

Lastly, you can learn a lot by asking your CEO directly, "What do you most need from us to make this organization succeed?"

Backed up by strong board support, your CEO just might spin that straw into strands of gold.

YOUR EVALUATION

12. Our board delivers on its promises to the CEO.

__ Strongly Agree __ Agree __ Disagree __ Strongly Disagree

13 ☑

Is our relationship with staff honest, collegial, and within appropriate boundaries?

According to the U.S. Bureau of Labor Statistics, U.S. companies lose $3 billion a year to the effects of negativity. Negativity leads to high absences and turnover, loss of creativity, low morale, and poor customer relations.

Nonprofit workplaces aren't exempt from ordinary business stresses. But we have another, deeper reason to stamp out negativity. How can we address the societal problems we encounter each day without a daily dose of optimism to replenish our souls? So let's wipe out one source of negativity – thorny board-staff relationships – and build collegial ones instead.

It pays to start at the top. The leadership style of your CEO is essential to board-staff harmony. Destructive board blaming can be nipped in the bud by CEOs who consult with staff, communicate honestly, and take personal responsibility for getting the job done.

But relying on the CEO exclusively for harmonious board-staff relations isn't wise. Both directors and staff benefit from face-to-face encounters.

At many organizations, staff and directors work jointly on projects – staff may support the directors in their governing role, other times directors assist staff as volunteers. Distances naturally close when you learn to appreciate each other by working together.

But be careful. When directors and staff work closely on common projects, it takes a fair amount of director discipline not to abuse your role by issuing orders – remember, supervising the staff is the CEO's job.

For staff who don't have the chance to interact in this way, directors and CEOs need to be deliberate about creating opportunities for directors to meet and talk with them. Director site visits are not only good for staff morale, they're also an excellent opportunity to see for yourself what's happening at your organization.

No matter how big or how small your organization, staff members appreciate boards that honor their accomplishments. There are ample opportunities for recognition, from issuing a congratulatory board resolution to joining celebrations of important staff milestones.

Overall, the Golden Rule works pretty well as a guideline for staff and board interaction.

YOUR EVALUATION

13. Our board has a productive and harmonious relationship with the staff.

__ Strongly Agree __ Agree __ Disagree __ Strongly Disagree

---

14 ☑

Does our board ask the right financial questions?

Which of the following describes your board when financial matters are discussed?

    a. Directors scrutinize spending in every line item and grill the CEO on any variances.

    b. Directors avoid eye contact with the treasurer and think *"I'm really glad Mary understands all this financial stuff."*

    c. Directors don't worry about a thing because their Executive Director has the finances under control.

There's a better way to approach financial matters.

    d. Directors review a concise report focusing on important financial targets, raise questions about any variances, and don't let the issue drop until they're satisfied corrective action will be taken.

Most of us have a love/hate relationship with all things financial. We love money, but hate to think about managing it.

How many of us stick to household budgets or follow long-term investment plans? (or have one?) And reading corporate financial reports – UGH, I'd rather eat worms!

Unfortunately, what you might get away with in your home isn't sufficient to carry out the fiduciary responsibility you have as a nonprofit board. Financial stewardship is a critical part of your duty.

You needn't be a certified public accountant to understand nonprofit finances. But you do need to learn enough to ask and answer the questions that matter.

When I worked at an international children's charity, our board used a handy tool to zero in on the most important financial indicators. We called it a top line report, others describe it as a 'dashboard.'

Each month, instead of scanning dozens of pages of financial data, our directors reviewed *one page* that reported on just 10 indicators. Every director, no matter how financially sophisticated, could see at a glance whether our $25 million organization was on target or not.

If an indicator was off, staff attached a report explaining what action was underway to fix the problem. Full data was still available as a backup to directors who wanted it.

Of course, the reason for knowing your financial

condition is so you can do something soon enough to keep your organization solvent. Surprisingly, too many boards confuse rigorous monitoring with taking corrective action.

YOUR EVALUATION

14. I understand and can verify our organization's financial condition.

__ Strongly Agree   __ Agree   __ Disagree   __ Strongly Disagree

---

15

Have we built
a secure financial base?

You can help financially bewildered directors become more adept if you define *fiduciary responsibility* with a few key questions.

1) *Do we have enough cash to pay the bills?*

More than a few organizations have months when they can't meet payroll or other bills. A cash flow budget would have warned them about problems in time to prepare solutions to those temporary fluctuations.

2) *Have we spent more than we have raised?*

An organization that reaches the end of the year without balancing its operating budget puts its future solvency at risk. If you routinely fund annual shortfalls from your reserves, in a few years you'll be out of existence.

3) *Do we honor donor intent? Have we done what we said we would do with the money?*

When you accept money from a donor with restrictions, *you can't use these funds for anything else.* If you solicited money for a particular purpose, you made a promise you have to keep. Responsible boards differentiate restricted obligations from other cash needs.

4) *Have we paid our taxes?*

Nonprofit organizations are always liable for payroll taxes. Some also incur sales, property or income taxes. I've heard too many stories of organizations that were paying both penalties and back payments when the IRS discovered they were misusing payroll taxes withheld from employees.

5) *Have we saved for a rainy day?*

Some directors mistakenly believe that nonprofits can't accumulate a surplus at the end of the year. You can. In fact, you need a reserve to manage cash flows or unexpected outlays.

How much reserve should you have? While experts suggest enough to cover a year's worth of expenses (don't laugh), most small organizations would be thrilled to have three months of unrestricted funds in reserve.

While it's not easy, one way to build that cushion over time is to make "transfer to reserves" a line item in your annual budget. And then to have the discipline to fund it.

•••

Your board may need to ask a few more financial

questions unique to your particular organization. But these five simple questions – which all directors can understand – are the starting point for building a secure financial base for every organization.

YOUR EVALUATION

15. Our board has prepared for the organization's current and long-term financial stability.

__ Strongly Agree __ Agree __ Disagree __ Strongly Disagree

---

16 ☑

Do we report our finances accurately to the public?

Media coverage of gross financial misreporting by major corporations shook public confidence – and resulted in stricter federal oversight. Even without government regulators snapping at their heels, trustworthy nonprofit boards will make sure their financial statements are in order.

Now I realize you selected your treasurer, chief financial officer or CEO because they can be trusted. You have complete confidence in their integrity.

Nevertheless, heed the words of the late Ronald Reagan – *"trust, but verify."* Even in the nonprofit world, financial abuses happen.

One of the best ways to verify your financial condition is by commissioning an annual *audit*. Prudent nonprofit boards are adopting the model legally required of corporations and placing their audits in the care of a board Audit Committee.

Audit Committees are, first and foremost, independent bodies. They forbid staff, paid consultants, or directors with conflicts from serving on them.

The committee oversees the process from top to bottom. It starts with selecting an auditor with nonprofit expertise and free of financial ties to the organization. And it ends with the presentation of a meticulous document to the board for approval.

Your annual revenues may already trigger the need for a full audit (check your state or provincial law to see whether this is the case). Also, some funders, including many foundations and the federal government, often have audit requirements you'll need to meet.

If an audit isn't mandatory and you genuinely can't afford one, consider paying for a less costly compilation or review. At the very least, periodically hire an accountant to assess how well your internal controls protect your organization from the likelihood of fraud or abuse.

An audit will also be useful when filing your federal tax return (Form 990). You're legally bound to make the 990 available to the public (it's readily available on the Internet). You'll have more confidence in its accuracy if the numbers are taken from your audit.

With increased public scrutiny and skepticism, nonprofit boards can no longer afford to be sloppy about their finances. Our unique nonprofit privileges are at stake.

YOUR EVALUATION

16. I am confident that our financial reports to the public are accurate and complete.

__ Strongly Agree __ Agree __ Disagree __ Strongly Disagree

17 ☑️

Are we getting accurate information?

It saddens me every time I learn about a scandal hitting a charity ... *CEO of highly respected social service agency indicted on multiple counts of fraud and mismanagement ... city inspectors find broken equipment endangers children at nonprofit child care center...*

Each time I read one of these stories, I ask, *what was the board doing? Didn't they know these problems were going on?*

Apparently not ... at least in some cases. But there are other boards, equally culpable, that mandate changes, yet fail to oversee them.

Responsible boards don't make wishful assumptions. Instead, they create rigorous monitoring systems to reassure themselves that everything is in order.

As to what is involved in setting up a system, let

me borrow here from board consultants, John and Miriam Carver.

The Carvers suggest three ways for boards to gain peace of mind:

1) Ask for a report.
2) Inspect for yourself.
3) Have an outsider conduct the inspection for you.

The best monitoring systems use a combination of all three methods. By way of example, let's use your organization's finances.

You're using method #1 if your CEO provides you with monthly financial statements, or completes the dashboard report we discussed in Chapter 14. CEO reporting is probably the most frequently used form of monitoring.

It works well enough when the board is *explicit* about the information it needs *and* if the person delivering the report is levelling with you.

But, as common sense dictates, the best way to verify accuracy is to inspect things for yourself – method #2. For example, you might delegate a director or two to examine bank statements or verify that employee payroll taxes were paid on time.

Finally, if you lack the expertise to evaluate, or if you want an independent review, you may need to use method #3 – the services of an outside expert. You already do this when hiring an accounting firm to conduct your audit or review your internal financial controls.

Monitoring not only guards against abuse, but it's the only real way to verify performance – of your CEO, your programs, even the board itself.

And considering your organization is entrusted to you, doing so is nothing less than your moral and legal responsibility.

YOUR EVALUATION

17. Our board verifies that the information we receive is accurate and that board mandates are carried out.

__ Strongly Agree __ Agree __ Disagree __ Strongly Disagree

18

Have we managed risks to our organization and its people?

When considering risk, adopt the Boy Scout motto – *Be Prepared*.

Boards are legally bound to exercise reasonable care (known as the "duty of care") when making decisions for their organization. Even the best insurance won't protect you when you're negligent.

Obviously, you can't avoid or even think of everything that could possibly go wrong. You'd never provide services to a client or hold an event if you tried to run your organization that way.

So instead, protect your organization by adopting a *risk management mindset*. You can do this by following the advice of The Nonprofit Risk Management Center:

- Inventory what might go wrong.
- Plan for how you'll prevent or respond to that potential harm.

* And should something bad happen, safeguard
  your organization from financial ruin.

The Center has grouped the risks organizations face
into four categories:

* People.
* Property.
* Income.
* Reputation.

These categories provide an excellent framework for
developing a risk management plan.

For example, have you considered the likelihood of
harm befalling staff, volunteers or donors at your gala
event? What if someone slipped and injured themselves
in a fall?

Certainly, you want to verify in advance of the event
that you, the venue, and your caterers are sufficiently
covered by up-to-date liability insurance. You'll want to
review safety procedures with everyone working at the
event. And, you might even recruit a roving clean-up crew
to mop up any missed spills.

Or what about your property? Are your computer
files backed up each day? Are those backups stored off
premises? Will your insurance cover the costly expense
of retrieving data in the event something should fail in
your backup plans (imagine the cost of retyping all of
that information)?

Your insurance company, the Nonprofit Risk
Management Center, and even professional associations

like the Public Relations Society of America can be instrumental in helping you figure out what to worry about and how to plan adequate safeguards.

YOUR EVALUATION

18. Our board can demonstrate our assets (tangible and intangible) are protected from fraud, abuse, or negligence.

__ Strongly Agree __ Agree __ Disagree __ Strongly Disagree

☑ 19

Do we prevent conflicts of interest from influencing decisions?

Good board stewards make decisions in the best interests of their organizations. Staff too.

Fraud or ethical scandals usually occur when directors (or staff) start acting in their own interests and not for the benefit of their organization.

Sometimes conflicts arise purely from board laziness or the desire not to offend a director. It's tempting to forgo outside bids when a director who is also an insurance agent offers to handle all of your insurance needs. Or the banker. Or the caterer.

You can't eliminate all conflicts of interest, especially in small communities. After all, you've recruited directors because they do have interests connected to particular constituents, business, government or other community organizations.

Still, because directors bring their interests with them,

your board must have a written conflict of interest policy spelling out in clear terms how to deal with real or perceived conflicts.

Typically such policies include:

• What defines a conflict of interest.

• How and when directors (and staff) are required to disclose any potential conflicts.

• Whether directors or their families are forbidden from engaging in any business transactions with the organization or if there are conditions under which these transactions could be allowed.

• What practices must be followed to ensure that any such business relationships meet the standards of an arms length transaction.

In evaluating complex conflict situations, a colleague of mine suggests you use the *New York Times* test. Ask yourself: How would our organization look to the public if this deal were reported on the front page of the morning paper?

Avoiding conflict of interest falls under a larger legal principle known as the "duty of loyalty," which requires directors always to base decisions on what's in the best interest of the organization.

It also obligates directors to safeguard confidential information – for example, not to secretly slip your donor list to another organization.

If directors hold their duty of loyalty dear, it should follow that they'll always act in your organization's best interest.

YOUR EVALUATION

19. Our board has sufficient controls in place to prevent director or staff self-dealing or conflicts of interest.

__ Strongly Agree   __ Agree   __ Disagree   __ Strongly Disagree

---

PART III

BUILDING A GREAT BOARD

"Talent wins games, but teamwork and
intelligence win championships."

Michael Jordan

20 ☑

How good is our board?

Until now we've talked about the work the board has to do – making a difference in the community and being good stewards of your organization's assets.

In the next few chapters you'll evaluate the strength of your board team and review how well you're working together. But before we get started, let's step back and look at the board, overall.

You probably have somewhere between five and 20 people on your board, perhaps more. They aren't paid, and still show up for somewhere between three and 24 meetings a year. Their combined volunteer hours probably total in the hundreds annually.

Knowing this, are you confident you're putting this prodigious resource to the best use? Do all those hours and all that talent add up to a powerfully positive force for your organization – something it would be absolutely lost without?

And if you went one by one to each of your directors,

would 100 percent of them say the hours they spend on behalf of your organization are well spent?

Would they describe their board experience as rewarding, important, even exciting?

I've worked with organizations that rarely lack for board recruits. These are boards on which it's a privilege to be asked to serve and where it's impossible to stay on the board if you don't perform. These are boards where staff would feel a great loss without their leadership and good counsel.

If this doesn't describe your board, it can – perhaps sooner than you think. You'll need a few strong partners among your directors with the will and the time to lead the reform. You'll have to speak up and help build new ways of working together. But it can be done. And you can do it.

YOUR EVALUATION

20. I feel a great sense of reward serving on this board.

__ Strongly Agree   __ Agree   __ Disagree   __ Strongly Disagree

---

21 ☑

Do we recruit the directors we want and need?

Being a director for your organization is a task only the special few are qualified to fulfill. You've got to believe this or you'll wind up with a disappointing board.

Boards shortchange themselves by trying to fill director jobs with a la carte people – a lawyer, an accountant, or a public relations professional – instead of searching for the right people to propel the organization forward.

Let's imagine a museum dedicated to the preservation of historic boats. Your work is internationally significant but your resources are limited and you're relatively unknown.

If you were describing two or three ideal board candidates for this museum, who would they be?

To build your international reputation, you'd probably want a few world-renowned experts on some aspect of your mission (there's nothing wrong with thinking big).

You'd want some directors to help build your financial base by making significant gifts and introducing you to other potential donors.

You may want special expertise in areas such as tourism, historic preservation, and nonprofit governance.

You'll also want geographic diversity and deep roots in boating.

Nary a person identified for being a lawyer or accountant, is there?

But if yours isn't a boat museum, how do you identify who you want and where to find them?

I'm familiar with an overseas relief organization that longed to secure more federal funding and build stronger relationships with its international partners. Standing in its way was a perceived lack of credibility on program issues – largely because it lacked directors with recognized expertise in the area.

So the board made a push for directors with experience and reputation in these matters. They scoured their donor list. They sought out faculty from respected universities. They asked their own professional contacts for referrals. They kept their eyes trained on newspapers, periodicals, and television stories.

And lo and behold, after several hits and more than a few misses, they found the candidates they needed.

You can follow their example. What are the

critical challenges you face? What ideal candidates would help meet those challenges?

Patiently pursue them. It's far preferable for the health of your organization than settling for the quick, easy ... and wrong pick.

YOUR EVALUATION

21. Our board nominates only those directors who meet carefully considered qualifications.

__ Strongly Agree __ Agree __ Disagree __ Strongly Disagree

22

Have we trained directors so that they can make a meaningful difference?

Supermarkets invest more in training the teenagers who run the cash registers than most nonprofits invest in training their directors.

I venture to say there's a lot more at stake when the board blunders than when the checkout kid does.

Every board needs to invest in director training – for both new and continuing directors. We've already discussed the ways to keep directors abreast of important trends and community changes. So let's turn our attention to the training needs of new directors.

Many individuals with great potential have never been on a board before, especially young people. Even if you have served on other boards, you're just as likely to have learned bad habits as good ones. It's better to set up your own training for your directors – then you control what they're learning.

The place to start training is during the recruitment

process. Before voting in new directors, be sure they've received sufficient background on your organization and their duties.

Having board candidates visit your site can be especially illuminating – to let them see your programs firsthand and to observe a board meeting in action. Included here can be an interview with the CEO and key staff with whom the candidate may be working closely.

Once on board, your new directors will benefit from a formal orientation program. Typically, it's here that new directors receive their Board Handbook, a binder containing your bylaws, mission, values statements, budget, policies and more. Have them sign for it to reinforce its importance and your expectation that directors come to meetings prepared.

At the orientation, new directors can meet committee chairs and hear about particular projects before choosing an assignment. New directors can also benefit from a board mentor. With the support of these senior members, new directors will be productive faster. Have them meet at the orientation.

When you design your training, ask your current directors what they wished they had known in those first days of their service. Then build that valuable advice into a better orientation program.

YOUR EVALUATION

22. Our education and training programs prepare us to contribute meaningfully.

__ Strongly Agree __ Agree __ Disagree __ Strongly Disagree

23

Do we follow our bylaws?

Recently two instances arose in my town that demonstrated the importance of bylaws.

In the first case, a small group of donors tried to stop the board of a nonprofit library from selling a rare book in its collection.

In the other, the firing of a popular CEO of a community action group led to a threatened lawsuit to nullify the vote and oust the board.

In each case, the disgruntled parties based their case on charges that the board had failed to act in accordance with the bylaws.

How well do your directors know these fundamental rules governing the operation of the board?

While no one expects directors to memorize every passage of their bylaws, it's not unreasonable to expect every director to be fluent in their most important provisions – such as rules for voting, nominations, quorum, or terms of service.

You can always verify what you can't remember by bringing your Board Handbook (which contains the by-laws) to the board meeting. There's no need for guessing.

Failure to follow your bylaws can invalidate board elections, diminish legal protections, or expose your organization and its directors to liability. It can also be a signal that your board isn't taking other responsibilities seriously either.

If your bylaws are outdated because your practices have evolved, then you should change them. When you do, here are a few points to keep in mind:

- Be scrupulous about following the process in your bylaws for changing your bylaws.

- Limit your bylaws to the most essential procedures. Less important ones can be placed in an easier to update policy manual. You'll appreciate the flexibility.

- Only list committees required by state law or those essential to board functioning (governance and audit committees, for example). Then, in your bylaws, delegate to the board the ability to create or disband other committees as needed.

- Because your bylaws are a legal document, have changes reviewed by legal counsel. Counsel can steer you away from unwise practices and ensure your bylaws conform to appropriate state and federal laws.

Changing your bylaws won't remedy problems per se, poor board performance, for example. However tempting it may be, you won't increase director commitment by lowering your quorum rule or dumbing down your organizational structure.

YOUR EVALUATION

23. Our board carefully observes the rules and procedures described in the bylaws.

__ Strongly Agree __ Agree __ Disagree __ Strongly Disagree

---

24 ☑

Do we make policy instead of one-time decisions?

Bylaws aren't the only rules governing your organization. Board *policies* also guide staff and board action.

Effective boards make policy rather than decisions. If that sounds confusing, let me make a distinction.

Decisions answer a particular question confronting us here and now. They often lack application to any future questions that might arise.

Policies, on the other hand, provide frameworks for making decisions that can be applied to future questions. Not only are they key to sound board decisions, but policies allow boards to more effectively delegate authority to others.

Here's an example:

Your well-known organization frequently receives offers from businesses interested in marketing opportunities. For example, a local bar would like to hold a promotion using your name and give you a percentage of the beer served that night.

Every time an offer like this arises, it goes to the board

for a decision. Largely because the reasons for accepting or rejecting are based on the likes and dislikes of the directors in the room that evening, tonight's decision may contradict one you made last month.

A better approach is for the board to streamline decision-making, ensure consistency, and even delegate more decisions to staff by creating a *policy* for this type of venture.

In this case, a marketing policy would outline the conditions needing to be met before such a deal would be acceptable, (e.g. minimum dollar guarantees, agreed payment schedules, written contracts, use of your name and logo, prohibited businesses or types of deals, and compliance with Better Business Bureau guidelines). Once in place, the next offer can be accepted or rejected in accordance with this policy.

Of course, policies only have value when they're followed. If the only record of your policies is in the meeting minutes, within a year or so no one will remember the details – or even if you made a policy at all.

You can improve board memory by incorporating each policy into a Policy Manual. Arrange the policies by topic, mark them with an adoption date, then tuck them into your board handbook, where they'll be readily available for future reference.

YOUR EVALUATION

24. Our board creates policies that guide future board and staff decisions.

__ Strongly Agree __ Agree __ Disagree __ Strongly Disagree

25 ☑

Does our board govern and resist the temptation to manage?

The board governs. Staff manages.

If only the line were so clear!

Creating and then observing the boundaries between board and staff roles requires a great deal of skill by boards and their CEOs.

But there are measures you can adopt.

Creating job descriptions and work plans for the board and its committees can help clarify board responsibilities.

Using policies, as discussed in the previous chapter, is a second way for boards to effectively delegate and reduce their inclination to meddle in staff business.

Even with safeguards, however, there are certain problem areas to be aware of. For example:

- Directors who are chief executives or top level

managers in their own workplaces are used to managing. They may have a hard time respecting the boundaries of their board position.

• Meetings that include detailed verbal reports from staff or committees tempt directors to offer staff advice on how to do their jobs – encouraging micromanagement.

• It's always tempting for directors to talk about trivial implementation questions – such as ways to save money on printing or what band should play at the upcoming gala. Instead, focus on questions of major importance, like developing a long-term, sustainable revenue plan for the organization.

While the chair of the board has the prime responsibility for keeping the board focused on substantive issues, all directors can share the responsibility.

If board conversation wanders inappropriately into staff territory, any director can pull it back – "it's always fun to talk about these things, but these are staff decisions. Let's get back to board work."

When directors do offer advice to the staff, remind those directors that staff have complete authority to accept or reject any advice that doesn't come in the form of a board-approved decision.

So why is this important? Director time is limited. When directors micro-manage, they shift attention away from the macro-level issues that are board's responsibility. They risk undermining staff morale with their meddling. And they undercut their own oversight responsibilities.

If your board is involved in management affairs, it will take attentive leadership and self-discipline to pull it back.

YOUR EVALUATION

25. Directors focus on board matters and do not inappropriately interfere in staff work.

__ Strongly Agree __ Agree __ Disagree __ Strongly Disagree

26

Do our committees improve the functioning of our board?

Draw a line down the middle of a piece of paper.

On the left side, list each of your board's standing committees. Now, on the right side, write down what each of those committees is expected to accomplish this year.

How did you do?

Directors can usually answer the first question. The second is the real test of committee effectiveness.

We ask so much of our directors and our staff that we shouldn't burden either of them with unnecessary work. I've attended many a committee meeting where directors passively listened to staff reports and then made minor suggestions. What a waste.

You don't need board committees simply to advise staff. You don't need committees to meet every month if they have nothing to do.

In assessing the value of your individual committees, ask yourself a few questions:

- Are our committee assignments aligned with our strategic plan?

- Do we really need to establish a full committee or could this project be completed by a time-limited task force?

- Do we dissolve committees when they're no longer needed (in accordance with your by-laws, of course)?

Committees are most valuable when they improve the effectiveness of the full board without usurping its authority to make decisions. They work best as mini think tanks that can summarize for the board the issues, options, and implications of various courses of action.

On the other hand, committees are detrimental when they make decisions that are rightly those of the full board or allow the board to abdicate its responsibility. Having a finance committee doesn't exempt the rest of the board from its fiscal responsibility.

Try limiting standing committees to the fewest needed. State or provincial law will advise whether you're required to have any standing committees at all.

What about an Executive Committee? Read on.

YOUR EVALUATION

26. Board committees advance the work of the board.

__ Strongly Agree __ Agree __ Disagree __ Strongly Disagree

27

Do we avoid rubber stamping and decision reworking?

You excitedly joined a new task force at work. Your boss shows up for the first meeting, tells you he met with his inner circle and has come up with a solution for you to approve.

You raise a few questions, but otherwise vote in favor because you really don't have another choice (short of updating your resume, that is). Oh, and by the way, you and your task force are 100 percent responsible for any problems resulting from the boss's decision.

How many times would this have to happen before you stopped volunteering for any new assignments?

Unfortunately, this rubber stamping scenario plays out at too many nonprofit board meetings. Want to eliminate it? Dissolve your Executive Committee. Yes, that's right, get rid of it.

Executive Committees are fraught with hazards. They create an in-group/out-group dynamic. They inappropriately issue directives to the CEO and make critical decisions in lieu of the full board.

All the while, the full but now disenfranchised board is still legally responsible for all decisions made by its executive committee.

Boards justify their executive committees as needed to deal with unexpected events between meetings. But just how many emergencies does a typical organization have?

If decisions can wait for a scheduled executive committee meeting, then surely (in all but extraordinary circumstances) they can wait for a scheduled board meeting, especially if the board meets monthly.

You may have a good reason for an executive committee – perhaps your board is spread across the globe and meets only three times a year. But even then, could today's email and teleconferencing technology offer alternatives?

•••

On the flip side of rubber stamping is another aggravation: decision-reworking. Does your board have difficulty finalizing decisions? Does it keep reopening decisions made meetings ago?

Some contributors to decision-reworking are poor board attendance, decision-making absent adequate information or discussion, lack of policies, failure of dissenters to speak up, or unskilled meeting leadership.

You are much less likely to find decisions being reopened when concerns have been well-aired and high levels of consensus achieved.

YOUR EVALUATION

27. Policies and substantive decisions are carefully considered and made by the full board, except in cases of extreme emergency.

__ Strongly Agree __ Agree __ Disagree __ Strongly Disagree

---

28 ☑

Are our meetings productive?

"Who called this meeting?
"We thought you did...
"Maybe meetings have become a life form capable of
calling themselves and reproducing via human hosts."

– from *Dilbert*, by Scott Adams

Why do so many people detest meetings? Because they spend so much time in bad ones.

It's hard to function as a board without meetings. While some jurisdictions may allow email voting, meetings are still the standard for board work.

Most of us recognize a good meeting. Our opinions matter. We learn something new and enjoy our colleagues. We don't waste time on trivial distractions.

If your meetings aren't like that, here are a few strategies that might help:

- Limit agenda items so that you have time to discuss substantive issues. And put the most important first.

- Banish oral reports (put them in writing and hold directors accountable for reading them). Insist that committees present only well-framed policy questions for consideration.

- Adopt practices that improve your deliberations. Maybe it's the old standby, "Robert's Rules of Order." Or, an alternative like "Quaker consensus" might suit you. Whatever method you choose, train your directors to use it.

- Use your top-line report to focus on important variances, and ignore distracting details.

- Build a mission-reinforcing or educational activity into each meeting. At our humanities council meetings, we begin by discussing a short story, poem, or article sent to directors in advance.

Still, your directors are likely to have different points of view on what makes a good meeting.

I've heard a few describe a good meeting as one ending in 60 minutes. Those boards were either extraordinarily disciplined or rarely discussed matters of substance.

You'll find common ground on meeting management if you have a frank discussion within your board on what works, what doesn't, and what changes directors would like to make.

YOUR EVALUATION

28. Board meetings focus on substantive issues that are critical for directors to discuss.

__ Strongly Agree __ Agree __ Disagree __ Strongly Disagree

29

Have 100 percent of our directors made a gift?

Let's not equivocate about this topic. In fact, let's be dogmatic. *Every single director of a nonprofit public charity should make a donation to their organization.* No exceptions.

You've may have heard these two common reasons for this:

- Funders, notably foundations and corporations, expect 100 percent board giving.

- Directors can't credibly ask others for money if they haven't made their own gifts first.

These are very good reasons, but I can cite instances where they weren't a factor. Money was raised anyway.

In my experience, there is a more pressing reason to expect directors to contribute. Unwillingness to give is a fairly reliable sign directors don't have the passion and commitment your organization needs.

Great directors feel the righteousness of your cause

in their head *and* in their hearts. They take their work seriously and know if they don't do it, no one else will.

Don't misunderstand. Charitable giving is a voluntary act. You can't coerce directors into giving. What I'm suggesting is that when you ask directors to serve, one of the obligations the *right* candidates will be willing to accept is the act of giving to your organization.

After all, if your directors, the people with the legal and moral responsibility, won't put their money to work for the organization, why should anyone else?

Remember the Mom test? Call this the Director test.

Now, when discussing board giving, an inevitable question arises: *Should we require directors to give a specific amount?*

Since many organizations can benefit from having directors from a wide variety of financial circumstances, it doesn't usually make sense to specify a certain level of gift.Even the poorest among us can and do give to the causes that matter to us.

If I were pinned down, I'd say ask your directors for a gift that reflects the depth of their commitment. It should be among their two or three most important gifts of the year.

How much? As my friend Herb Kaplan says, *give until you feel good.*

YOUR EVALUATION

29. I am confident that all board members make a personally meaningful financial contribution.

__ Strongly Agree   __ Agree   __ Disagree   __ Strongly Disagree

---

30

Have we decided the board's role in fundraising?

I can't think of another issue that causes as much anguish at nonprofit organizations. Countless books and seminars are devoted to this subject. Staff complaints about director failures in this area are commonplace.

It is a widely-accepted axiom that a critical duty of nonprofit boards is to raise money. But if this is such a given, why is it such a problem?

I myself am convinced that board fundraising isn't a truism. Throughout the nonprofit world, you'll readily find examples of highly successful organizations where virtually all fundraising is done by staff.

Does the board have an obligation in resource development? Absolutely. It starts with the one we've already discussed: building an organization that's worthy and trustworthy of support. Without this, it's hard to be to be successful raising money.

And the board is also responsible for making sure the organization has the resources to get the job done – today, and in the future. That includes deciding what types of revenues, how much and in what proportion. It also means deciding *who* is to generate those funds.

Most boards delegate to staff fundraising tasks that require specialized skills – jobs like direct marketing, grant writing, or planned giving.

But where staff is at a disadvantage is in opening doors to potential funders, be they philanthropic individuals, business leaders, or even government officials.

Here, directors often have more legitimacy and clout as volunteers, colleagues, friends, and community leaders themselves.

Opening doors can naturally lead to asking prospects for money, and herein lies the source of conflict – the point of contention – between boards and staff.

If your revenue plan depends on this personal work, *someone has to do it.* There is no right answer as to *who?* Your board gets to decide.

You can decide directors aren't obligated to open doors or raise money, and hand this responsibility entirely to staff. And there is plenty of precedent for this. Just do so knowing what services or outcomes you may be sacrificing.

If you choose to have directors involved, then it's critical to train them well, provide support, and hold them accountable for the obligation they've taken on.

Unfortunately, tens of thousands of nonprofit organizations aren't raising very much money at all. Could it be they're still arguing about the directors' role?

YOUR EVALUATION

30. Our board has decided which fundraising responsibilities, if any, we will hold ourselves accountable for.

__ Strongly Agree __ Agree __ Disagree __ Strongly Disagree

---

31 ☑

Do we have a way to evaluate our own performance as a board?

There are many ways to evaluate board performance: at an annual retreat, at a board meeting, or one-on-one with individual directors. All three make a nice package. Let's discuss each in turn.

• *Retreats*

Many boards review their performance at a special full- or half-day gathering set aside for that purpose. A questionnaire asking directors to rate the board against a number of key indicators (*see the Appendix*) can help guide the discussion.

On the plus side, retreats offer a concentrated period of time to focus on one question. They build bonds between directors by allowing time to socialize and become more comfortable working together. People usually feel energized when they leave.

On the downside, too many boards wait to hold retreats until a crisis occurs, or the board is barely functioning. Then directors mistakenly assume a retreat is the panacea. But it's unrealistic to expect one full or half day will repair what the board failed to do in its year of working together.

* *Board meetings*

It's best if your board has time throughout the year to discuss its performance. That way, emerging problems can be rapidly addressed. Consider reserving some time at a meeting every quarter or semi-annually to review how the board is working and design strategies for improvement.

If your board needs help talking about its performance, a neutral third party can help structure the discussions. Ask organizations you trust to recommend a qualified consultant.

* *One-on-one*

Another important aspect of board evaluation is checking in with each director, one-on-one, at least once a year. These personal conversations can alert your leadership to any problems and help a non-performing director become active again (or wean them off the board).

Whatever evaluation method you use, the end product should be a list of ways to improve your performance. Some will address significant issues, others minor irritants.

So that the entire exerise isn't in vain, ask a particular director or two to champion a particular improvement (for example, designing and implementing a director education program).

That way, you're more likely to make progress.

YOUR EVALUATION

31. The board conducts a thorough evaluation of its own performance at least once-a-year.

__ Strongly Agree __ Agree __ Disagree __ Strongly Disagree

32

Have we made board excellence someone's priority?

To create a great board team, it helps to make someone responsible for the care and feeding of the board and its directors.

For most organizations, this defaults to the board chair, adding an enormous responsibility to this already demanding job.

In organizations where no one is attending to the board, the CEO usually steps in. This isn't desirable either as it turns the board-CEO relationship on its head.

There is another solution. More organizations are expanding the task of the nominating committee to include other aspects of board development. Renamed the board's *governance committee*, this revitalized group is often asked to oversee the following:

• *Director education*

This includes new director orientation but also other training throughout the year.

• *Director and board evaluation*

The governance committee ensures that individual directors and the board as a whole are evaluated annually.

• *Leadership transitions*

You may have been on a board where no one wanted to be president so it defaulted to the person who was least resistant. An untrained or disinterested president can wreak havoc on board functioning. Boards that consciously groom future officers benefit from the stronger leadership such attention brings.

• *Committee development*

The governance committee can help the board determine when to create new committees or when to terminate those no longer needed. It can also nominate committee chairs and help those chairs round out the committee, with non-board volunteers if necessary.

Other responsibilities for this committee include *updating board job descriptions, overseeing board mentoring* or *recognizing director* accomplishments.

While the governance committee needn't be large, its responsibilities, as you can see, are important enough that it should meet year round.

YOUR EVALUATION

32. The board has a functioning committee responsible for evaluating and improving board performance.

__ Strongly Agree __ Agree __ Disagree __ Strongly Disagree

33

Do we appreciate our directors for what they do?

Humans are social creatures. Our ancient tribal instincts drive us to form and join groups.

And wow, do we ever! Beyond the family, and extended family, we have book groups, motorcycle clubs, online discussion groups, cooking clubs, chat rooms, faith-based organizations, alumni associations, sports teams – the possibilities for grouping are endless.

With so many choices and so little free time, why should anyone belong to a group that doesn't bring them joy or fulfillment?

Let's face it, your board is just another group. And when you ask someone to join, you're asking that person to choose the board over another way to spend hours of their time. You have to make sure it's worth it to them.

Providing rewarding work is the primary way. But

close on its heels is appreciating directors for the work they do.

A colleague recently shared this story. A health problem, coupled with a board disagreement, prompted an extraordinarily hard working director to cut back her service.

But rather than let her fade away, the board surprised her at an annual gathering with a simple award: her photo blown-up and labeled our "Champion."

This special appreciation was just enough to rejuvenate the director's passion and now she's back to her old super-volunteer self.

When deciding upon your own forms of recognition, stay with ideas appropriate for your organization. A community garden, for instance, might present directors with the inexpensive gift of a basil seedling at a spring meeting.

For its popular Daffodil Day fundraiser, one state division of the American Cancer Society loaned its best performing local board a striking painting of the flower.

Some groups are even more creative. I've heard of organizations that send a letter of appreciation to the director's spouse and kids honoring their sacrifice.

While it seems obvious, many organizations forget to send their departing directors into the world with a hearty "thank you."

For example, I recently attended an annual meeting where nary a word of appreciation was offered for a director rotating off after six years of service. What a shame – and potential loss of someone who very well could be a lifelong advocate and volunteer.

Boards that nourish and nurture their directors never lack for candidates for board service. Word gets around.

YOUR EVALUATION

33. Directors feel appreciated for their service to the board.

__ Strongly Agree __ Agree __ Disagree __ Strongly Disagree

---

34 ☑

Do we act with courage and conviction?

I love the *Wizard of Oz* – what a great movie! This classic bursts with lessons for all ages:

- No matter how far you travel, there is no place like home.
- Good friends are a treasure to cherish.
- There's nothing like common sense.
- Be skeptical of authority.

And for nonprofit boards:

- If you care, you'll find the courage to overcome the impossible.

When you signed up for board service, you took on a hefty job, which you've read about throughout this book.

One thing the recruiting committee may have

forgotten to tell you is that it takes a lot of *courage* to serve on a board.

Why?

Leadership isn't easy. When we sign on for board service, we know that sometimes boards have to take on unpleasant tasks, like cutting budgets that result in staff or service layoffs, or even terminating a failing CEO or fellow director.

But the routine activities of a director also require a great deal of courage, like ...

... asking a question – when you're new and no one else does. And persisting till you get an answer you understand.

... suggesting it's time to do things differently from the way you always have. Or dissenting – especially when you're the only one.

... reaching out to your friends, family, colleagues or even strangers to ask for their help, especially if you are asking for their money.

... and critically and honestly assessing your own performance.

You don't have to be extraordinarily brave to be courageous. The cowardly lion's courage came from a great team, a strong belief, and a powerful cause. Does this sound like your board?

Just remember, like Dorothy, you don't need a room

full of superheroes to accomplish great things.

... Just heart
... hard work
... the nerve

YOUR EVALUATION

34. I have the courage to act for the good of the organization, above all else.

__ Strongly Agree __ Agree __ Disagree __ Strongly Disagree

Dedication

I've spent most of my life working in and volunteering for nonprofits. It has truly been a calling for me and I can't imagine my life's work having taken shape in any other way.

There is much to improve among nonprofit boards. Because the work is so important to the people we serve, we hold high standards for board performance.

Yet, it's easy to forget that directors of charitable organizations do the work they do without expectation of monetary reward. Heck, few are even lucky to get their mileage reimbursed!

While we strive for the stars, there is much to celebrate. Voluntary philanthropy brings us PTAs, youth sports leagues, music, theatre, dance, therapeutic riding, animal rescue, civil and human rights defense, women and children's advocacy, community development, international service, environmental protection, think tanks, universities, preschools, and too many other benefits to name.

To you who share large parts of your lives in service to the rest of us, *Thank You* from the bottom of my heart for caring enough to try to make your communities and our world a more vibrant, peaceful, and joyous place to live.

The Author

Gayle L. Gifford is a provocative writer, respected consultant, creative strategist, and long-time advocate for peace and justice. For Gayle, nonprofits are a promise to their communities, a societal commitment to create a better life full of hope, beauty, promise and equal opportunity for all.

Gayle believes that each nonprofit has an obligation to deliver on its commitment. In her work, she helps organizations be wise stewards of all of their resources - including their programs, their funding, their environment, and the human beings they touch.

Gayle brings her decades of experience at nonprofits small and large as a founder, director, volunteer, and senior manager to her consulting work with nonprofit boards and staff.

Gayle is a regular columnist for *Contributions* magazine and a respected contributor to online discussions on philanthropy. She is author of *Meaningful Participation: An Activist's Guide to Collaborative Policy-making* and co-author of *Bringing a Development Director on Board.*

When she's not working, Gayle can be found enjoying the many pleasures of her adopted state of Rhode Island and its capital, Providence, where she lives with her other passions – her husband and children.

Glossary

Director
Director refers to the official voting members of the board of directors. In some nonprofits, directors are also called trustees.

Chair of Board
This term describes the board's top volunteer position. Some organizations use the title, 'president.'

Because the term president is sometimes used by organizations to describe their CEO, I use Chair of Board to avoid confusion.

CEO
I've used the term CEO or chief executive officer throughout the book to refer to the top staff position in a nonprofit. Many call this person the Executive Director.

If you serve on the board of an organization without staff, the chapters on board and staff, or board and CEO, relationships won't apply.

But even here, your board should still hold itself accountable for the three yardsticks discussed in this book.

Nonprofit Organization
While boards of many nongovernmental organizations may find much of value in this book, I've written it from the perspective of nonprofit organizations which in the U.S. are known as "public charities."

In this country, a public charity is a type of nonprofit organization under section 501(c)3 of the tax code. It meets the requirement of having large and varied sources of support (as opposed to a private foundation, whose sources of support are relatively limited).

APPENDIX

About the Evaluation Survey

While every board can benefit from an honest evaluation, how to conduct that process is an organization-by-organization decision.

You might seek a reflective place for a formal one- or two-day retreat – perhaps at a conference center if yours is a major institution, or for smaller groups your director's kitchen table or cozy back porch may be all you need.

Then too, you might use one of your regular board meetings for the exercise, identifying one or two directors to guide the discussion.

Whatever the method, formal or informal, brief or extended, responding candidly to the statements on the following pages will be worthwhile.

On those issues where you "Strongly Agree," little action will be needed. You've laid a solid foundation. But take note of those areas where you "Disagree" or "Strongly Disagree."

Here is precisely where this survey will prove most illuminating and where you stand to strengthen your organization most markedly.

[PLEASE GO TO THE NEXT PAGE]

Evaluation Survey

Please respond to each of the following statements (these are the same ones appearing at the end of each chapter). Take time to think and reflect on your practice. *Candid* responses will be the most helpful to your organization.

1) Our board has articulated a vision and mission that are important today.
   __ Strongly agree __ Agree __ Disagree __ Strongly disagree

2) Our board has defined concrete results for the community change we will hold ourselves accountable for.
   __ Strongly agree __ Agree __ Disagree __ Strongly disagree

3) Our board regularly conducts/reviews research to gain a better understanding of our community and its needs.
   __ Strongly agree __ Agree __ Disagree __ Strongly disagree

4) Our board has clearly articulated the values that guide our decisions and actions.
   __ Strongly agree __ Agree __ Disagree __ Strongly disagree

5) Our board regularly considers the effects outside changes could have on the organization.
   __ Strongly agree __ Agree __ Disagree __ Strongly disagree

6) Our board regularly discusses how to create breakthroughs.
   __ Strongly agree __ Agree __ Disagree __ Strongly disagree

7) Our board is able to measure whether our organization is having a signficant impact on the community.
   __ Strongly agree __ Agree __ Disagree __ Strongly disagree

8) Our board has identified the tangible and intangible assets of our organization that need to be protected or grown.

__ Strongly agree   __ Agree   __ Disagree   __ Strongly disagree

9) I would feel confident letting my mother make a significant gift to our organization.

__ Strongly agree   __ Agree   __ Disagree   __ Strongly disagree

10) I am confident we have the right CEO for our organizaton.

__ Strongly agree   __ Agree   __ Disagree   __ Strongly disagree

11) Our board has clearly stated its expectations of the CEO and regularly discusses with him or her how well those expectations are being met.

__ Strongly agree   __ Agree   __ Disagree   __ Strongly disagree

12) Our board delivers on its promises to the CEO.

__ Strongly agree   __ Agree   __ Disagree   __ Strongly disagree

13) Our board has a productive and harmonious relationship with the staff.

__ Strongly agree   __ Agree   __ Disagree   __ Strongly disagree

14) I understand and can verify our organization's financial condition.

__ Strongly agree   __ Agree   __ Disagree   __ Strongly disagree

15) Our board has prepared for the organization's current and long-term financial stability.

__ Strongly agree   __ Agree   __ Disagree   __ Strongly disagree

16) I am confident that our financial reports to the public are accurate and complete.

__ Strongly agree   __ Agree   __ Disagree   __ Strongly disagree

17) Our board verifies that the information we receive is accurate and that board mandates are carried out.

__ Strongly agree __ Agree __ Disagree __ Strongly disagree

18) Our board can demonstrate that our assets (tangible and intangible) are protected from fraud, abuse, or negligence.

__ Strongly agree __ Agree __ Disagree __ Strongly disagree

19) Our board has sufficient controls in place to prevent director or staff self-dealing or conflicts of interest.

__ Strongly agree __ Agree __ Disagree __ Strongly disagree

20) I feel a great sense of reward serving on this board.

__ Strongly agree __ Agree __ Disagree __ Strongly disagree

21) Our board nominates only those directors who meet carefully considered qualifications.

__ Strongly agree __ Agree __ Disagree __ Strongly disagree

22) Our education and training programs prepare us to contribute meaningfully.

__ Strongly agree __ Agree __ Disagree __ Strongly disagree

23) Our board carefully observes the rules and procedures described in the bylaws.

__ Strongly agree __ Agree __ Disagree __ Strongly disagree

24) Our board creates policies that guide future board and staff decisions.

__ Strongly agree __ Agree __ Disagree __ Strongly disagree

25) Directors focus on board matters and do not inappropriately interfere in staff work.

__ Strongly agree __ Agree __ Disagree __ Strongly disagree

26) Board committees advance the work of the board.

__ Strongly agree   __ Agree   __ Disagree   __ Strongly disagree

27) Policies and substantive decisions are carefully considered and made by the full board, except in cases of extreme emergency.

__ Strongly agree   __ Agree   __ Disagree   __ Strongly disagree

28) Board meetings focus on substantive issues that are critical for directors to discuss.

__ Strongly agree   __ Agree   __ Disagree   __ Strongly disagree

29) I am confident that all board members make a personally meaningful financial contribution.

__ Strongly agree   __ Agree   __ Disagree   __ Strongly disagree

30) Our board has decided which fundraising responsibilities, if any, we will hold ourselves accountable for.

__ Strongly agree   __ Agree   __ Disagree   __ Strongly disagree

31) The board conducts a thorough evaluation of its own performance at least once-a-year.

__ Strongly agree   __ Agree   __ Disagree   __ Strongly disagree

32) The board has a functioning committee responsible for evaluating and improving board performance.

__ Strongly agree   __ Agree   __ Disagree   __ Strongly disagree

33) Directors feel appreciated for their service to the board.

__ Strongly agree   __ Agree   __ Disagree   __ Strongly disagree

34) I have the courage to act for the good of the organization, above all else.

__ Strongly agree   __ Agree   __ Disagree   __ Strongly disagree

Fund Raising Realities
Every Board Member Must Face
A 1-Hour Crash Course on Raising Major Gifts
David Lansdowne, 112 pp. $24.95. (*Bulk discounts available*)

If every board member of every nonprofit organization across America read this book, it's no exaggeration to say that millions upon millions of additional dollars would be raised.

How could it be otherwise when, after spending just *one* hour with this gem, board members everywhere would understand virtually everything they need to know about raising major gifts. Not more, not less. Just exactly what they need to do to be successful.

In this landmark book, David Lansdowne has distilled the essence of major gifts fund raising, put it in the context of 47 "realities," and delivered it in unfailingly clear prose.

Nothing about this book will intimidate board members. It is brief, concise, easy to read, and free of all jargon. Further, it is a work that motivates, showing as it does just how doable raising big money is.

Put this book in your board's hands, put it in your board orientation packet, put it anywhere you need the successful practice of fund raising masterfully illuminated.

ASKING
A 59-Minute Guide to Everything Board Members, Volunteers, and Staff Must Know to Secure the Gift
Jerold Panas, 112 pp., $24.95. (*Bulk discounts available*)

It ranks right up there with public speaking. Nearly all of us fear it. And yet it is critical to our success. *Asking for money.* It makes even the stout-hearted quiver.

But now comes a new book, *Asking: A 59-Minute Guide to Everything Board Members, Staff and Volunteers Must Know to Secure the Gift.* And short of a medical elixir, it's the next best thing for emboldening you, your board members and volunteers to ask with skill, finesse ... and powerful results.

Jerold Panas, who as a staff person, board member and volunteer has secured gifts ranging from $50 to $50 million, understands the art of asking perhaps better than anyone in America.

He knows what makes donors tick, he's intimately familiar with the anxieties of board members, and he fully understands the frustrations and exigencies of staff.

All of this knowledge and experience he has harnessed to produce the authoritative book on the subject.

What *Asking* convincingly shows — and one reason staff will applaud the book and board members will devour it — is that it doesn't take stellar communication skills to be an effective asker.

Nearly everyone, regardless of their persuasive ability, can become an effective fundraiser if they follow a few step-by-step guidelines outlined brilliantly by the master himself.

The Ultimate Board Member's Book
A 1-Hour Guide to Understanding and Fulfilling Your Role and Responsibilities
Kay Sprinkel Grace, 120 pp., $24.95. (*Bulk discounts available*)

Here is a book for all of your board members:

- Those needing an orientation to the unique responsibilities of a nonprofit board member,
- Those wishing to clarify exactly what their individual role is,
- Those hoping to fulfill their charge with maximum effectiveness.

Kay Sprinkel Grace's perceptive work will take board members only one hour to read, and yet they'll come away from The *Ultimate Board Member's Book* with a firm command of just what they need to do to help their *(Continued)* organization succeed.

It's all here in 120 tightly organized and jargon-free pages: how boards work, what the job entails, the time commitment involved, the role of staff, serving on committees and task forces, fundraising responsibilities, conflicts of interest, group decision-making, effective recruiting, de-enlisting board members, board self-evaluation, and more.

In sum, everything a board member needs to know to serve knowledgeably is here.

The Ultimate Board Member's Book is 'real world,' not theoretical, concrete not abstract. It focuses on the issues and concerns that all board members will inevitably face. As such, the book would:

- Nicely augment an organization's board orientation packet,
- Offer sound guidance to a nominating or board development committee,
- Clarify expectations for any board candidate considering joining your organization.

The Ultimate Board Member's Book has become *the* book in America to which organizations turn to ground their board members in the necessities of effective service.

The Fundraising Habits
of Supremely Successful Boards
A 59-Minute Guide to Assuring Your Organization's Future

Jerold Panas, 112 pp., $24.95 (*Bulk discounts available*)

Over the course of a storied career, Jerold Panas has worked with literally thousands of boards, from those governing the toniest of prep schools to those spearheading the local Y. He has counseled foundering groups; he has been the wind beneath the wings of boards whose organizations have soared.

In fact, it's a safe bet that Panas has observed more boards at work than perhaps anyone in America, all the while helping them to surpass their campaign goals of $100,000 to $100 million.

Funnel every ounce of that experience and wisdom into a single book and what you have is *The Fundraising Habits of Supremely Successful Boards*, the brilliant culmination of what Panas has learned firsthand about boards who excel at the task of resource development.

Habits offers a panoply of habits any board would be wise to cultivate. Some are specific, with measurable outcomes. Others are more intangible, with Panas seeking to impart an attitude of success.

Fundraising Mistakes that Bedevil All Boards (and Staff Too)
A 1-Hour Guide to Identifying and Overcoming Obstacles to Your Success

Kay Sprinkel Grace, 112 pp., $24.95 (*Bulk discounts available*)

Fundraising mistakes are a thing of the past. Or, rather, there's no excuse for making a mistake anymore.

And that goes for board members, staff, novice, or veteran.

If you blunder from now on, it's simply evidence you haven't read *Fundraising Mistakes*, in which one of America's notable consultants exposes *all* of the costly errors that thwart us time and again.

The special appeal of this book is that in one place it gathers and discusses the "Top 40" mistakes. Some you'll recognize, some you won't. But all of them you'll be happy to dispense with.

Just as anyone involved in journalism should own a copy of Strunk and White's, *The Elements of Style*, anyone involved in fundraising – board member, staff, volunteer – should have *Fundraising Mistakes that Bedevil All Boards (and Staffs)* by their side.

Copies of this book are available from the
publisher at discount when purchased in
quantity for boards of directors or staff.

Emerson
& Church
PUBLISHERS

Emerson & Church, Publishers
P.O. Box 338, Medfield, MA 02052
Tel. 508-359-0019 • Fax 508-359-2703
www.emersonandchurch.com